Finding Patterns

Food Patterns

by Nathan Olson

Capstone press®

Mankato, Minnesota

A+ Books are published by Capstone Press,
151 Good Counsel Drive, P.O. Box 669, Mankato, Minnesota 56002.
www.capstonepress.com

Printed in the United States of America in Stevens Point, Wisconsin.
122009
005645R

Library of Congress Cataloging-in-Publication Data
Olson, Nathan.
    Food patterns / by Nathan Olson.
    p. cm.—(A+ finding patterns)
    Summary: "Simple text and color photographs introduce different kinds of food patterns"—Provided by publisher.
    Includes bibliographical references and index.
    ISBN-13: 978-0-7368-6729-0 (hardcover)
    ISBN-10: 0-7368-6729-5 (hardcover)
    ISBN-13: 978-0-7368-7847-0 (softcover pbk.)
    ISBN-10: 0-7368-7847-5 (softcover pbk.)
    1. Pattern perception—Juvenile literature. 2. Food—Miscellanea—Juvenile literature. I. Title. II. Series.
BF294.O54 2007
516'.15—dc22
                                       2006018195

Credits

Jenny Marks, editor; Renée Doyle, designer; Charlene Deyle, photo researcher; Scott Thoms, photo editor

Photo Credits

Capstone Press/Gary Sundermeyer, 10; Capstone Press/Karon Dubke, cover, 14–15, 18; Corbis/Bill Varie, 22; Corbis/Envision, 6; Corbis/John and Lisa Merrill, 26–27; Corbis/Randy O'Rourke, 17; Getty Images Inc./Iconica/Bryan Mullennix, 4–5; Getty Images Inc./Iconica/Peter Miller, 25; Getty Images Inc./Photographer's Choice/Michael Rosenfeld, 19; Getty Images Inc./Taxi/Chris Alack, 11; Getty Images Inc./The Image Bank/Karen Beard, 16; Index Stock Imagery/Dennis Lane, 12–13; Index Stock Imagery/IPS Agency, 9; Shutterstock/Alex Balako, 24; Shutterstock/Christina Richards, 8; Shutterstock/Ingvald Kaldhussater, 20; Shutterstock/Krista Mackey, 29; Shutterstock/Laila Kazakevica, 21; Shutterstock/Larysa Dodz, 7; Shutterstock/Mary Terriberry, cover (peppermints), 1 (peppermints); Shutterstock/Myrthe Krook, 23

Note to Parents, Teachers, and Librarians

Finding Patterns uses color photographs and a nonfiction format to introduce readers to seeing patterns in the real world. *Food Patterns* is designed to be read aloud to a pre-reader, or to be read independently by an early reader. Images and activities encourage mathematical thinking in early readers and listeners. The book encourages further learning by including the following sections: Table of Contents, Food Pattern Facts, Glossary, Read More, Internet Sites, and Index. Early readers may need assistance using these features.

Table of Contents

What Is a Pattern?

Tasty treats with a repeating shape or color make a pattern. Let's look for patterns in all kinds of foods.

The yummy red and pink layers of a parfait make a colorful striped pattern.

Ice cream swirled with fudge makes a sweet dessert, but it doesn't make a pattern.

Meal Patterns

Before they're fried or scrambled for breakfast, fresh white eggs line up in a pattern.

Warm, toasted waffles repeat a crunchy pattern of squares.

Hot dog! Wavy squirts of ketchup and mustard make a lunchtime pattern.

Potato chips' rippled ridges form crispy, crunchy patterns.

This sizzling-hot dinner of steaks has a pattern of char lines.

Sweet Patterns

Soft and chewy gummy bears line up in colorful all-the-same and every-other patterns.

Frosted sugar cookies stack up in a sweet pattern.

Criss-crossed strips of pie crust make a pattern called lattice.

Sweet, bright layers of
red, white, and blue make
an icy-cool pattern.

A pattern of tiny squares covers the ice cream's cone. Can you guess why it's called a waffle cone?

Fruit and Vegetable Patterns

An orange's juicy triangles join in a fruity circle pattern.

Shiny ripe apples make an every-other pattern in the grass.

Tiny black seeds make
a circular pattern inside
a tasty green kiwifruit.

A tomato is a fruit too.
Vines of tomatoes grow
in a zigzag pattern.

Chop! A sliced onion shows
a perfect pattern of rings.

What's hidden inside a pea pod? A crunchy, sweet pattern of fresh green peas!

Food can make all kinds of tasty patterns. What patterns did you eat today?

Food Pattern Facts

Lattice top pies are as nice to look at as they are to eat. The top crust is made by weaving strips of pie crust dough over and under across the top of the pie filling.

Gummy bears are a chewy kind of candy shaped like little teddy bears. This candy originally was made in Germany where it is called *gummibär*, which means rubber bear.

Early American colonists refused to eat potatoes of any kind, thinking they shortened a person's life. Today, Americans eat more potato chips than people in any other country in the world.

What are those dark lines on meat cooked on a grill? They are called char lines. They happen when the meat sits on the hot iron bars of the grill. The char lines are a good sign that the fire is hot enough to cook the meat thoroughly.

According to legend, the first ice cream cone was made at the World's Fair in St. Louis, Missouri. A cookie seller rolled his wafflelike cookies into cone shapes. An ice cream seller topped the cones with his ice cream.

In the 1880s, a man named George Renninger invented candy corn. He filled small candy molds with three colors of corn starch. The pattern of three colored layers made the candy look like a kernel of corn.

Glossary

char line (CHAHR LINE)—a line burned into a piece of grilled food

circular (SUR-kyuh-luhr)—flat and round like a circle

criss-cross (KRISS-krawss)—a pattern of lines that cross each other

kiwifruit (KEE-wee-froot)—a small, round fruit with brown, fuzzy skin and green flesh

lattice (LAT-iss)—a pattern formed by strips that cross each other diagonally

layer (LAY-ur)—a single thickness of something

parfait (pahr-FEY)—a dessert made of alternating layers served in a tall, narrow glass

pod (POD)—a long case that holds the seeds of certain plants, such as peas

ridge (RIJ)—a narrow raised strip

sizzle (SIZ-uhl)—to make a hissing noise; steaks sizzle when they are grilled.

Read More

Bullard, Lisa. *Red Food Fun.* A+ Eat Your Colors. Mankato, Minn.: Capstone Press, 2006.

Ganeri, Anita. *Food Chains.* Nature's Patterns. Chicago: Heinemann, 2004.

McGrath, Barbara Barbieri. *The M&M's Brand Color Pattern Book.* Watertown, Mass.: Charlesbridge, 2002.

Internet Sites

FactHound offers a safe, fun way to find Internet sites related to this book. All of the sites on FactHound have been researched by our staff.

Here's how:

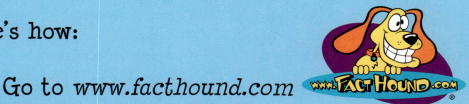

1. Go to www.facthound.com
2. Select your grade level.
3. Type in this book ID **0736867295** for age-appropriate sites. You may also browse subjects by clicking on the letters, or by clicking on pictures and words
4. Click on the **Fetch It** button.

FactHound will fetch the best sites for you!

Index